The Beast Under My Bed

by Julie Taylor

Illustrated by Sholto Walker

Wednesday 11th August, 4.00pm

Hi. My name is Karen. I'm writing this as a warning to you in case IT gets me.

If it does get me and you read this, you might know what to do and be saved.

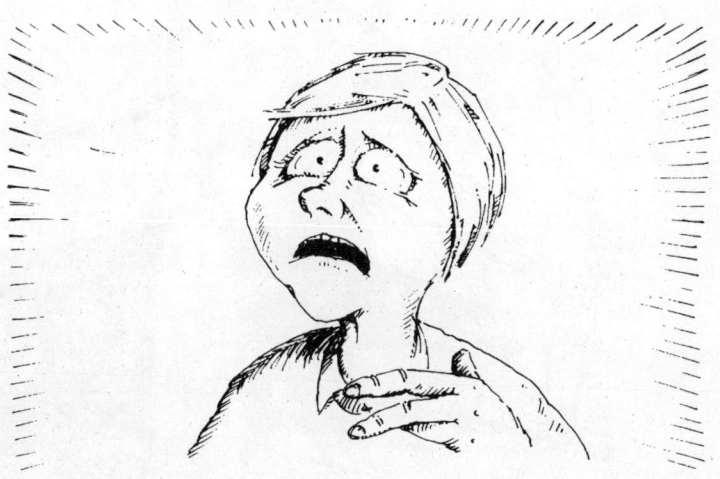

I came home from school today to find my mum had nipped out to the shops. I am all alone in the house. Well, that's not quite true. There is something else here in the house with me. It's under my bed right now ... waiting.

I know it's there. I've seen it.

Would it help if I told you

what it looks like? It is large – the

largest one I've ever seen – with

big beady eyes. Eyes that watch

me, as it waits for its chance. And

it's hairy. Very hairy. It has a huge

mouth with the biggest fangs I've

ever seen. One bite and ...

The thing is, I don't know what to do with the Beast. I know someone who does – my dad. But he's not here. He's away working and won't be back until Friday 13th.

I suppose I'll just have to wait until then and hope the Beast doesn't get me first.

Well, I'm going upstairs now, to get changed out of my school uniform. If I don't come back down again, you know it got me.

Just remember who warned you. Me. Karen.

Wednesday 11th August, 4.30pm

I'm back. I'm safe. But you'll know that, won't you? How else could I write this diary?

You'll want to know what happened, I suppose. How did I manage to get upstairs, get changed and come back down again without the Beast getting me?

Simple!

I opened my bedroom door and threw a blanket over the edge of the bed to stop the Beast getting out. Then I ran into the bedroom, grabbed my clothes and ran back out again. I went into the bathroom and got changed there. Clever, eh?

Right, I'm off out to see my
friends now. So I'm safe for a
while. What worries me most is
tonight, bedtime, when I'm alone
in the dark with the Beast.

Tell you what, I'll take my
diary to bed with me and make
notes. So you can learn in case I
make a mistake and it gets me.

Wednesday 11th August, 6.30pm

Hi. I'm back home. Yes, I did have a good time, thank you very much. Mum is home now so I'm not alone in the house.

I asked my friends to come in, but they wouldn't. Maybe I shouldn't have told them about the Beast under my bed.

Time to have tea now, then watch TV. Don't worry, I'll keep my diary close by in case the Beast escapes and I have to write and tell you what to do.

Wednesday 11th August, 10.00pm

Time has flown by. Mum says I have to go to bed now. I asked if it was all right to stay up late, but she said no.

Morning seems a long way off and I haven't even gone to bed yet.

In the bathroom I took my time brushing my teeth and getting washed. After all, if the Beast gets me I want to look my best when I'm found.

Mum is shouting, telling me it's time I was in bed – or else!

Well, here goes.

I feel cold all over. The bed is only two metres away. Three strides. All I need is the courage to move.

Three long strides. I'm going to throw the diary on the bed, then I'll do it. Then I'll run those three long strides and leap on to the bed before the Beast has a chance to get me.

Made it! I made it! I'm on the bed.

I've tucked the blankets round me and left the light on. I'm hoping the Beast won't come out while the light is on.

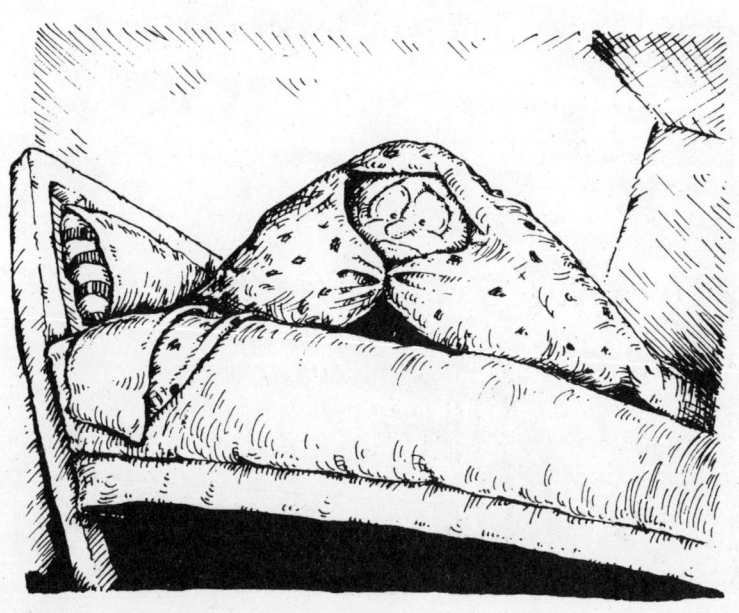

Thursday 12th August, 8.00am

Phew! That was close. I woke up during the night with my arm hanging out of the bed. I'm lucky the Beast didn't grab me with those huge fangs and gobble me up! I tucked my arm back inside pretty quick!

I suppose it's still under my bed,

unless it escaped during the night.

I'm not getting out of this bed until

I know where it has gone.

Well, I'm going to have a look.

Keep your fingers crossed for me.

I saw it! It's still there, staring

right back at me with those huge

eyes. All the food it had is gone

and I'm sure it's grown bigger.

Much bigger!

I can hear the Beast moving about. Maybe it thinks I will make a tasty meal. I think I'd better go and find it something to eat, quick.

That's better. I threw the Beast some scraps of food and it has calmed down.

Right, time for school now. See you later.

Thursday 12th August, 4.00pm

At long last. Some days you think they will never let you out of school.

Mum is in the kitchen getting tea ready. She's singing along to some soppy love song on the radio. Yuk!

No, I haven't been upstairs yet.

Give me a chance! I bet the Beast ○
is still there though, waiting.

Problem. I have homework to ○
do on the computer, and you can
guess where the computer is. ○

That's right, upstairs in my room.

I wish Dad would come home early. Tomorrow seems such a long way off with that thing under my bed. All sorts of things could happen to me by then.

I wish I could ask Mum to help, but she's terrified of her own shadow. Imagine what she'd do if she saw the Beast!

Thursday 12th August, 5.00pm

Tea is over. I'm not looking forward to going up to my room, but here goes. I've got some food for the Beast. With any luck the food will keep it happy while I'm doing my homework.

Here goes ...

○ Yes! I fed it and it seems quiet.

I'll do my homework.

○ Fast.

Thursday 12th August, 9.30pm

Oh, my! Look at the time. It's flown by. Before long it will be bedtime. Please let me be safe. It's only for one more night.

I suppose I'd better get ready for bed before Mum starts shouting at me.

Roll on tomorrow night. At least I'll be able to get a good night's sleep. If the hairy Beast doesn't get me first.

Look at it. It's huge!

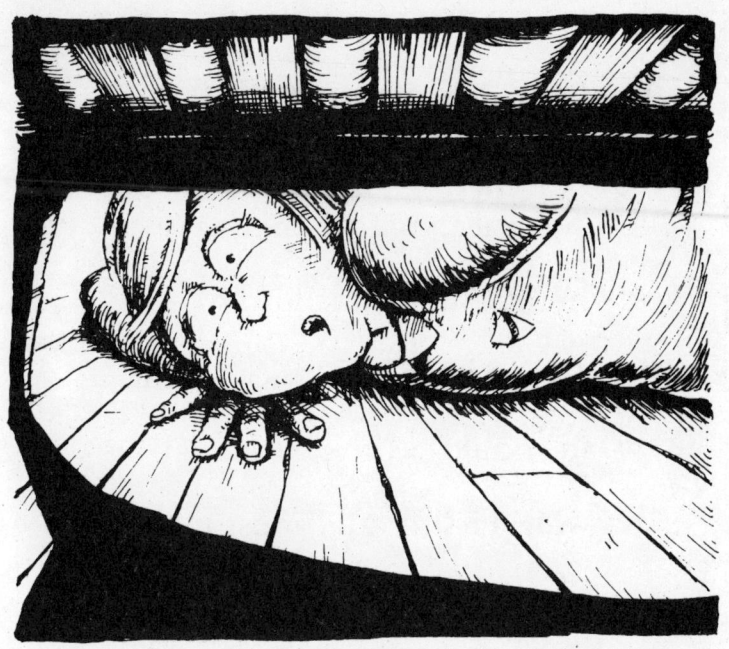

I'm sure it has grown even more. Its mouth is gigantic. Just think how big those fangs are now. I don't want to go to bed yet. I think I'll just sit in the chair for a while.

Friday 13th August, 7.30am

Oh! I fell asleep on the chair. My body hurts! At last it is Friday 13th. I hope it isn't unlucky for me.

Dad should be home today. I can't wait. First of all I must live long enough without the Beast getting me.

I feel sick.

Breakfast time and Dad is not here yet.

I wonder why he's late?

He'd better be coming home today. I don't think I can sleep with that thing under my bed for another night.

A car on the drive. It must be Dad.

It is! I'll help him in with his
case and tell him all about it. He'll ○
be able to sort the Beast out, then
we'll all be safe. ○

"Hi, Dad."

○

"Hello, Karen. Is everything ○
all right?"

"No, but it soon will be." ○

"What do you mean?"

"There's a Beast under my bed. It's been there since Wednesday and I need you to do something with it before it escapes."

"This had better not be another of your fancy daydreams, young lady."

"No. Honest. Mum knows all about it, but she's too scared to help. You know what Mum is like."

"Yes. OK, sweetheart," Dad smiles. "I'll have a look for you." ◯

I follow Dad to my room and hide behind the door. ◯

"Under here, is it?" he asks. ◯

"Yes, Dad. I want rid of it. I've ◯ hardly been able to sleep at night, wondering if it would escape and ◯ get me. Be careful!"

"I will. You wait there while I sort it out." He smiles and shakes his head.

"OK."

I can picture it now. My brave dad crawling on hands and knees under the bed. I wait for the scream as the beast bites him, swallows him alive.

Dad does scream. His legs jerk about as he struggles to get out from under the bed in a hurry.

I want to run, to get away, but I have to stay and watch my dad take the beast away.

"Fantastic," says Dad. "A Tarantula!"

"Urgh. Happy birthday, Dad. Just keep it away from me. I hate spiders."

Well, it seems as if you are safe after all. Thanks to me, Karen. I hope you're grateful.